SOMETIMES I WISH IT COULD ALWAYS BE DAY

Deji Ajibade

First published in Great Britain as a
softback original in 2022

Copyright © 'The Roaring Lion Newcastle'
The moral right of the author has been asserted.
All rights reserved.

No part of this publication may be reproduced, stored in a retrieval system, or transmitted, in any form or by any means, without the prior permission in writing of the author, nor be otherwise circulated in any form of binding or cover other than that in which it is published and without a similar condition including this condition being imposed on the subsequent purchaser.

Cover Design: Buzz Designz

Published by 'The Roaring Lion Newcastle'
ISBN: 978-1-913636-84-5
eISBN: 978-1-913636-85-2

Email:
books@theroaringlionnewcastle.com

Website:
www.theroaringlionnewcastle.com

ALSO, BY Deji Ajibade from
The Roaring Lion Newcastle'

"Living By The Script: Making The Most of
Your Life" (A collection
of Inspirational and Motivational Essays)

Dedication

This book is dedicated to God Almighty, the giver of life and destiny.
And also to the memory of my parents, Mr. Adebomi and Mrs. Anike Ajibade, who have been called home by their creator.

Acknowledgements

A big thank you to the editors of the journals below, for giving my poems their first abode.

'My Shepherd and I' first appeared in *Agape Review*.

'Awakening' first appeared in *The Kolkata Arts*.

This is to acknowledge some great individuals whose immense contributions to the success of this book I cannot go without mentioning.

I would like to thank my parents, Mr. and Mrs. Gabriel Akinyemi, who have filled a great vacuum since I was a little boy. I sincerely appreciate your endless support and love, Dad and Mum. In fact, words cannot express my gratitude to you enough.

I thankfully acknowledge the support and inspiration given to me by my brother and mentor, Tolu' A. Akinyemi, while writing this collection of poems. Your time and other resources deployed to support the production of this book are well appreciated.

My profound gratitude equally goes to the editor, Diane Donovan, for finessing this collection into a complete body of work. Your input is well appreciated.

I specially thank my supportive wife and daughter, Sarah and Tiwatope, for always believing in me. Thank you for always encouraging me to do more. You know I love you, ladies.

Finally, I acknowledge with gratitude all my family and friends, innumerable to mention, who supported me in one way or the other in making this a reality. You guys mean a lot to me.

Contents

Children of Dust and Dirt (Black) 2
Magic of Transformation (Climate) 3
Grief 5
My Shepherd and I 6
Sometimes I Wish It Could Always Be Day .. 7
Even In War, There Is Hierarchy 8
My Son 9
In The Belly Of Woeful Nights 10
The Falling 11
Awakening 12
Superman 13
There Are Nights 15
Like 2020 16
Not Giving Up 17
Ode To This Mother 18
Through the Thin 19
Here, Hope Will Not Die! 20
Metamorphosis 21
Endless Dreams 22
Dry Leaves 23
Tapestry 24

Portrait of Love	25
Redemption	27
Finding The Lost Coin	28
Summation	30
The Other Face Of Love	31
The Baptism	32
Rosary	33
Explosion	34
Ojo (Day)	35
Homelessness	36
Falling Stars	37
Lies	38

POEMS

Children of Dust and Dirt (Black)

To the children of mahogany skin and charcoal black eyelids, I say power. To the children snatched from the wake of a fairy tale and tossed into the harshness of a nightmare, I say power. To the children wrapped with a ragged shawl at birth and fed crumbs of bread to survive the daily scourge of want, I say power. Power to you, children of dust and dirt, for we still can rise. From the ashes of burnt dreams, we still can rise; from the charred remains of slaughtered hope, we still can rise. Rise and face the East; see the sun smiling on you, cheering you to a day of reawakening where you hold your fate in your hands and weave it into an embroidery of hope. Power to you, children: the Earth is your victory field.

Magic of Transformation (Climate)

Man has always expanded beyond himself;
he wrought the magic of transformations, a little god.
It's how thick forests become cities and riverbeds, estates.
But, in his expansion, he desecrates nature;
goes beyond his boundaries in his drive for innovation.
His factories set the sun on fire.
He feeds the ocean with dirt and
razes down forest trees.

And now, the heat wave is killing,
and waters that once gave life are now emissaries of
diseases and death.
Floods make a wreckage of homes, and storms
destroy cities

Pray tell, when shall we arrive at a green world?
When will waste be recycled instead of being dumped
in our oceans,
when will we treat the trees as sacred and save the sun
from the emissions,
dark as a swarm of locusts?

We need to save the world and stop the plundering of nature
before we become casualties of our own deeds.

Grief

in order for grief to win a body, it cages it in loneliness:
to be sad and have no one to talk to;
to need company and yet lack the will to seek it.

self-destruction has never thrived when there's closure: no,
the shadow of death lurks in dark places and strikes in lonely corners,
and yet, grief is hardly ever painted on the face.

My Shepherd and I

I asked the Lord,
"Who are you?"
He said, "I'm a map leading you into places
God has intended you to be.
I'm the light flooding your path with illumination and the
still voice of guidance."

And then I know.
I'll never regret making Jesus my Shepherd.

Sometimes I Wish It Could Always Be Day

in my dreams i still see
the body my brother left behind, shawled in dust
and Father's retreating shadow.

sometimes i wish it could always be day
and all the lights of heaven would never go to sleep,

for, in the depths of the night,
my dreams carry me to dark places:
ravaged cities that echo with grief and
hasty departures,
places that smell like my mother.

in my dreams, i wear Isa's shirts and sing
Jimmy Cliff along with my father while
Mother worries about us disturbing the neighbours.

when i wake up, i pick the old guitar
and cling to the strings of memory.

Even In War, There Is Hierarchy

Every man was equal until bombs began to make homes
desolate.
Our cities were overtaken, and places where we once made memories became mountains of rubble.

We left home behind to find refuge in foreign lands.
But, at the border, skin colors were grouped into hierarchies:
Whites first, Blacks maybe...

But I've seen blood ooze from different shades of melanin,
and it's crimson—all crimson.
I've seen women in a unison of tears, and
Brotherhood formed to fight certain death.
But there, at that border,
some skins are worth more than others.

My Son

My Son, there are cities you should not visit,
streets littered with naked pixels that set your mind aflame
with lust.
There, your heart is a slave to fleeting feelings,
infatuations that derail you from your purpose.

There, you forget the sound wisdom of your mother,
the time-honoured words of your father.
You soil the sanctity of your mind and desecrate the temple of
your body.

My son, make a covenant with your eyes:
fix them on the Word of your Lord and the purpose he's set before
you.
Free your mind from ensnarement and it'll become a theatre of
beautiful things.

In The Belly Of Woeful Nights

There are times when your body shrinks from you,
Your mind receding into a sea of dark thoughts.
There are days your mind wishes it has legs.
Perhaps then it'd run to heaven.

Some nights are barren of the moon and stars,
When fireflies don't grace the indigo carpets of the sky.
They are nights that remind you of the dreams you've lost,
Nights that echo with voices calling you a failure.

When you're buried in the belly of these nights,
Reach out to the heavens, and you'll touch the face of God.
Fill your mind with songs of his love and your limbs
Will be graced with the strength to overcome.

The Falling

Time never lingered, not even for a second.
She ran, arms wide, as if competing with the wind.
She ran, flooding my mind with pressure to compete with her.
She ran, plunging me into palpitations until the Lord blew
calmness and the
sun cheered hope.
Say the pressure fell for peace—
A peace that words can't capture;
the peace that diluted time's speed in
seconds, before my eyes;
the peace that suppressed pressure, propelled energy, and broke down the walls of restlessness.
It was then that I could wait for life to play fairly, for peace
cords my heart.

Awakening

to the monster named anarchy
the mother of corruption   the son of
perdition   the dark clouds swimming
in the sky   drying off honey and raining
dust   the thief that erases meats and feeds
us with crumps   you monster   we've known
you for the rag you are   the truth has
unmasked your
face and we see you're a demon roaring like a
lion   we see
your shadow struggling with our freedom
but we'll show you
iron is made of irons   we'll show you dark
clouds don't linger
all day   then   the trees will dance at our
awakening   it shall
record the sons of the soil shaking off specks
of dust and
grabbing
their possessions

Superman

i
the first time you allowed a chicken to live
after tasting death, a heave rolled off your shoulders.
it'd been winking at you, seducing your teeth to
transverse its finesse.

ii
you cleared the choking path of the
naira notes in your mum's purse like
light in the wilderness; allowed their tongues
to taste another, glorifying the god of greed.

iii
your belly sang lullabies to
the candies in your mum's
cupboards; the candies kept
for your brother.

iv
like every life that's subject to
growth, your wings grew into fraud. you
call yourself an activist fighting for reparation—
"White men planted religion and reaped your father's gold."

v
mumbo jumbo!
boy, you wanted a lamb. you allowed
darkness wrap your thought like before the beginning

of creation, but now your whole life has become a night behind
bars.
who will save you, superman?

There Are Nights

   my thoughts wander like
      a lost sheep searching for
         her siblings. those nights, sleep
becomes
            a metaphor; a metaphor too fragile
               to hold. what's the word for
loneliness
               that cages peace? i wonder if
loneliness is a seed, if
      it grows like the
      trees. sometimes my head is a movie
displaying all scenes
       ever seen. i could exit this world
      with the bottle of pills lying on the floor
and my body on the
       other side of the room, my body broken
into smithereens,
       floating into oblivion. i wonder if God
sees us from up there?
       mayhaps, a cavalry could save me from
the voices in my
       head. they get so loud, i wish i could
shoot them out.
       Dear God, if
       you're out there, help me. there are
nights when my head
       wallows in
       unrest. if you're there, sail me in peace.

Like 2020

It's 2022,
just like 2020, too,
when sleep sailed too
far from the eyes, when a plague
plundered the earth, when doors refused to
blink 'cause of the lockdown, when black skin
cried 'till death strolled him off, knees bent under
a car; when our hearts prayed for a miracle the most.

It's 2022,
just like 2020 too.
He's caught in the rain, in Ukraine,
where black skins glow fear and rejection.
Today, you are the first black man to cure the blind;
Tomorrow the soldier is too blind to see you're a man.
Your black skin rumbles hate in him.
It's 2022,
but not like 2020, 'cause we won't
watch melanin-glowing skins cry
from reception anymore. we'll speak
and speak and speak 'till equity is brought
to the forefront.

Not Giving Up

Time ticks thoughtlessly
Leaving regrets uphill.
My heart squeezes.
Dawn seems far.

When I look into the sky
The birds fly without boundaries
With no place to call home when it rains.
I wonder how they keep warm and wait for the sun
To finally sing their beautiful songs.

It is a cliché
That there's light at the end of the tunnel.
I choose to light up that tunnel
To spark a fire and warm my cold soul
To go beyond the express
Though its route is rough.

What rhythm makes noise
Nothing less than trouble?
So I'll make it lyrical
And will hit my highest note.

Ode To This Mother

This mother is fading away. See
how her skin is hardened with
drought, her seas barren and
gray. See how disasters are subtracting
her once-daunting figure into a silhouette, into
restlessness, into destitution. No wonder her
fruits are slim like brooms, like streaks of tears. See
how her once-soothing songs are receding into
whispers. See
how her green is washing off. No wonder her
fruits are slim like brooms, like streaks of tears.
We sucked Mother
Earth's breast, yet grew to stab her with dirt and
pollution. We encountered
her care, yet grew to bite her nipples. She fell to
her knees, chewing every insult
as curds. She sacrificed her health for our
pleasure, yet we thickened our ears from
her faint cries of help. We have stabbed her, but
we can resurrect her like Lazarus. We
should wipe her tears, reapply her makeup, and
watch her spread a smile again. We can. Mother
Earth deserves better.

Through the Thin

Another brown sweat greets the ground, and my gaze falls on the terrace.
The mud polished on my palms breaks like departing walls and fatigue colours my sight.
The toil is transfiguring into normalcy and my slow steps outline the muddy tracks.
I'm sucking in these tears and am trying to calm the
storm erupting inside. How work determines to drain humans. How the quest to make ends meet
push us to dire limits. Lullabies to these pains: I've walked
through this thin world for so long. Lullabies to these pains: I
don't need
another pair of eyes to see the green flag smiling at me. I won't unroll
myself. Lullabies to these pains: my eyes are too glued to the prize.

Here, Hope Will Not Die!

we shroud hope in withering hands
and water our seeds with tears and
prayers. we cloak ourselves in broken songs, hoping
they'll reach the ears of heaven,
but our longings are wingless birds; they are slaves to gravity
so, for a bountiful harvest, we reap the remnants of locusts.

but here, hope will not die
though each day greets us with fresh pains,
hope will not die.

we will sow and sow until the earth yields her increase for us.
until our barns overflow with the children of our seeds
we will rise each day, clinging to hope.

though our hearts break now,
the sun shall rise from the east bearing healing in its rays.

Metamorphosis

what's the word for an ant once in a dark-lit
web, nursing pains and anxiety and curses from
her children and the greed of her leaders? what

do you call an ant once punctuated with
corruption and deceit and massacre and everything
named recession? an ant scourged with

colonialism— the mother of disruption. an ant
winged with failures and grief and more failures, but
breaking out of all of the stenches like a thunder from

lightening bolts. Say her citizens rise like
some phoenix from the ashes and hold the sun from barren
 lands. Say
her citizens raise her flag of wealth, of greenness, of culture, of
 unity. Say that the ant
metamorphoses into the giant of Africa she's called. Say her
brilliance floods the world like wildfire and baptizes everyone with
awe. Say the rejected stone becomes the chief cornerstone.

Endless Dreams

smoke from mosquito coil...
twists of my
endless dreams

Dry Leaves

dry leaves falling
on drought—
climate change

Tapestry

What holds the heart from
Falling into brokeness like streaks of
Tears? Or, what propels its flight in smiles
If not love? Since the day my eyes locked with
Yours at the restaurant, since the day we exchanged contacts and
Laughed with each other, I knew the sweet taste of attraction.
My heart still thumps your personality, propels the flight of
Smiles across my face. My mind colours your face everywhere,
In every dream; rewinds your voice in every silence. Every dew
Refreshes
The cords connecting our hearts with understanding sprouts
Chills at
The mention of your name, Emabong.

Portrait of Love

What is left of a shadow if she keeps sifting into

Misconception and grief? Ever since my heart weaved with

Wale's, my mind dropped love like a chimney housing heartaches; heaving

Frustration. My mind dropped love as a scalpel camouflaging silver in silhouettes.

Wale would crown our arguments with the "silent treatment," flinging me into inferiority. Wale

Would bathe me with insults in the morning, flirt with chicks in the afternoon, force our bodies to twirl

In embroidery in the night. Imagine me on the window pane, counting aches like numbers. Imagine me on

The window pane caressing my wounds with tears, performing an autopsy with bottled losses. Imagine me

Nursing pain in a dark-lit room, yet covering it with smiles and makeup and clothes and good words. What do you

Call pretence, in your language? If not for therapy and friends' help, I wouldn't have seen love's real face.

Now I see that love is the hand that knits understanding between two hearts. I see that love is the bubble that flaunts

Sacrifice like the sky flaunts clouds. I see that love isn't about exploring sex, moans defiling the air. I see that

Love is the seed that sprouts into care and intelligence, like a tree.

I see that love is the cloth that cleanses sins and

Grief and tears. I see love, and my face tastes joy again.

Redemption

long night...
my sweats meets
my tears for redemption

Finding The Lost Coin

"... real faith passes through the body like an arrow"
~Kaveh Akbar

I'd heard of miracles— the cloning of bread and fishes into

thousands, the walking in sea as if it were a rug of sands, the

transformation of an ignored colt to the chief of the day, dead

eyes blinking after a prayer ... but they rung like fairy tales, like

Cinderella fantasies, like flowers looking real ... but upon holding, it

It withers away. Say, my brain couldn't hold onto a mystery named God;

my faith, a lost coin until life sifted its vanity onto me, bombarding

my face with its frivolity. Until life leveraged failure at my footsteps,

I had to search for faith like a lost coin. I'd subscribe to redemption.

It was then that I realized that faith isn't a mirage. It was then that I tasted miracles

and saw they're sweeter than potatoes.

Summation

1 + 1 equals the white
rattling dark noses with the
wealth of their skin; equals
dark noses begging for spaces to breathe; for
voices to ride on; for justice, as if she's wandered
away like a chimney's smoke.

1 + 1 equals hatred blanketing hearts, birthing
arguments and strife and blood flowing like flood;
equals stealthy walks from fear of the next attack
instead of 1 culture and 1 system and 1 skin and 1 mindset
clashing with another culture and system and mindset like two
opposite claws. where's the face of love? have we all forsaken
her like a refuse dump? we can't taste her fragrance, for once, at
least?
when will 1 + 1 equal the unity we're craving for?

The Other Face Of Love

You say love is
the dew that burns
that it's the heat
that quickens longings, that
births attraction and
imaginations and everything
beautiful. But you never told me love has another
face— the face that drills aches in the heart,
that demands sacrifices.
You didn't tell me that
there are nights when tears that will lure me to sleep.
you didn't tell me the other face of
love requests patience in unbuttoning
misunderstandings. you didn't tell me. you didn't.

The Baptism

another bomb baptizes
a sea of bodies, transforming their
smiles to cries rising as incense
to the god of terrorism. say that a bomb
licks treasures. ashes flowed at the
day's wake, but before then, one of
the treasures, before being forced to
walk death's lane, tweeted for help, but
insults covered the response. what's the solution
to a country leaking failure like a punctured tube?
what do we do to green the green of this fading country?
treasures were lost, cries rose as incense and a smile
transverse the terrorists' faces for "success".

Rosary

rosary circles...
staring to find answers
before wolves appear like sheep

Explosion

fire explosion...
congregation struggling with
life and death

Ojo (Day)

Did you see how yesterday
disgorged failure from her
 chimney?
Did you see?
I set out today again, like

a pregnant rain, loading myself with the blessings of
fruitfulness. I have knitted kindness

with my customers and pitched my business on the
roof of a skyscraper. I beckon to passersby with honeyed tongue.

Ojo, please unfurl fruitfulness to me.
It is a must that earth heeds the chameleon's wishes—
I speak to you today, Ojo, Unfurl fruitfulness, Ojo.
Unfurl fruitfulness and let my purse be full again.

Homelessness

night stroll...
the homelessness of
fallen leaves

Falling Stars

night stroll...
the trail of falling
stars

Lies

fly around like
the wandering wind, throwing
some noses into mud, keeping
some minds from mouthing the
truth, erupting confusion as a volcano,
and wrapping some hearts with uncertainties
about the truth. But the truth, like a seed in the
soil, will crawl out again. Shoot him hundred
and a thousand and a million times. Tilt his
limbs, break
his head, do your worst. The truth cannot bleed
to
death. He can't taste death. Do your worst: he can't
taste death.

Author's Note

Thank you for the time you have taken to read this book. I hope you enjoyed the poems in it.

If you loved the book and have a minute to spare, I would appreciate a short review on the page or site where you bought it. I greatly appreciate your help in promoting my work. Reviews from readers like you make a huge difference in helping new readers choose a book.

Thank you!

Deji Ajibade

Author's Bio

Deji Ajibade is a Nigerian-born writer. He holds a master's degree in clinical psychology from the prestigious Obafemi Awolowo University in Nigeria.

He is passionate about and dedicated to using counselling to help people navigate through everyday life issues and ensure that they lead more productive lives.

Deji actively trades in foreign exchange in the world of finance. He's also a lover of nature and the arts.

www.ingramcontent.com/pod-product-compliance
Lightning Source LLC
Chambersburg PA
CBHW021453080526
44588CB00009B/824